A CourseGuide for

Tactics

I0191567

Gregory Koukl

ZONDERVAN
REFLECTIVE

ZONDERVAN REFLECTIVE

A CourseGuide for Tactics

Copyright © 2019 by Zondervan

Requests for information should be addressed to:
Zondervan, *3900 Sparks Dr. SE, Grand Rapids, Michigan 49546*

ISBN 978-0-310-11104-7 (softcover)

Printed in the United States of America

CONTENTS

Introduction

Welcome to *A CourseGuide for Tactics*. These guides were created for formal and informal students alike who want to engage deeper in biblical, theological, or ministry studies. We hope this guide will provide an opportunity for you to grow not only in your understanding, but also in your faith.

How to Use This Guide

This guide is meant to be used in conjunction with the book *Tactics* and its corresponding videos, *Tactics Video Study*. After you have read each chapter in the book and watched the accompanying video lesson, the materials in this guide will help you review and assess what you have learned. Application-oriented questions are included as well. For additional practice, you will want to complete exercises found in *Tactics Study Guide*.

Each CourseGuide has been individually designed to best equip you in your studies, but in general, you can expect the following components. Most CourseGuides begin every chapter with a "You Should Know" section, which highlights key terminology, people, and facts to remember. This section serves as a helpful summary for directing your studies. Reflection questions, typically two to three per chapter, prompt you to summarize key points you've learned. Discussion questions invite you to an even deeper level of engagement. Finally, most chapters will end with a short quiz to test your retention. You can find the answer key to each quiz at the bottom of the page following it.

For Further Study

CourseGuides accompany books and videos from some of the world's top biblical and theological scholars. They may be used independently, or in small groups or classrooms, offering quality instruction to equip students for academic and ministry pursuits. If you would like to engage in further study with Zondervan's CourseGuides, the full lineup may be viewed online. After completing your studies with *A CourseGuide for Tactics*, we recommend moving on to *A CourseGuide for Seeking Allah, Finding Jesus; A CourseGuide for Apologetics at the Cross;* and *A CourseGuide for Cultural Apologetics*.

Learning the Columbo Tactic (Chapters 1–3)

You Should Know

- "What do you mean by that?" is the first apologetics question to ask to gather facts with genuine interest, providing a natural opening for no-pressure conversations.

- Respond to the statement "It's not rational to believe in God" by asking: "What do you mean by 'God'; what kind do you reject? Specifically, what's irrational about believing in God?"

- Respond to the statement "Christianity is basically the same as all other religions" by asking: "How much have you studied other religions to compare the details and find a common theme?"

- Respond to the statement "You can't take the Bible too seriously because it was only written by men" by asking: "Is there a reason you think the Bible is less truthful or reliable than other books you own? Can you explain?"

- Respond to the statement "It's wrong to force your views on other people" by asking: "When you vote for someone, wouldn't that essentially be forcing your views on others?"

- Apologetics: Apologists defend the faith, defeat false ideas, and destroy speculations raised up against the knowledge of God.

- Ambassador Model: This approach trades more on friendly curiosity than on confrontation, using a kind of relaxed diplomacy to sharing Christ.

- Offensive apologetics: makes a positive case for Christianity by offering evidence

- Defensive apologetics: answers challenges to Christianity like attacks on the Bible, answering the problem of evil, or dealing with Darwinian macroevolution

- Columbo tactic: going on the offensive in an inoffensive way, using carefully selected questions to productively advance conversations about Christianity

Essay Questions

Short

1. Consider Greg's story about his encounter with the witch while on vacation in Wisconsin. What did you think about this encounter, and the way he engaged her in conversation? Was there anything that stood out to you? If so, what?

2. Greg reminds us that the tool available at our disposal to aid in our observations of the world and helps us separate fact from fiction is God's gift of reason. How do you think Christians have neglected this tool in the past? How might it look to steward this tool in your own conversations about the Christian faith?

3. Reflect on the 100% God and 100% Man principle, as outlined on page 37. How does this reshape for you what it means and how it looks to evangelize and engage in spiritual conversations?

4. How should the realization that "you don't have to try to close every deal" impact how you converse with people about your faith?

5. What do you think about the question, "What do you mean by that?" In what way is this a natural opening for a conversation, and how do you think it would help your spiritual conversations with people you know?

6. What do you think about the Columbo approach to apologetics and spiritual conversations outlined in this lesson? List some of the advantages you feel this approach has, especially as compared with other approaches you've experienced.

Long

1. Consider each of the scenarios outlined on pages 42–43. Pick one, and explain how you yourself would have responded. Then, share how the insights from this lesson on the Columbo tactic could help you navigate such conversations.

2. Read Mark 2:1–12, Luke 20:1–8, and Luke 20–26. What did you notice about the way Jesus engaged his opponents in spiritual conversations? How can you combine those insights with what you've learned in this lesson to inform how you talk about your faith?

Quiz

1. Rather than looking like an all-out D-Day war, how should our apologetic engagements look?

   a) Like a walk in the park
   b) Like an effort at diplomacy
   c) Like a waste of time
   d) Like we've won

2. What approach to apologetics is more about friendly curiosity — a kind of relaxed diplomacy — than on confrontation?

   a) Conversion Model
   b) Persuasion Model
   c) Servant Model
   d) Ambassador Model

3. What three basic skills are required of every Christian when representing Christ in the new millennium?

   a) Knowledge, wisdom, and persuasion
   b) Knowledge, wisdom, and character
   c) Gifts, wisdom, and character
   d) Knowledge, revelation, and character

4. What do apologetical tactics require?

   a) Careful listening
   b) A thoughtful response

    c) Paying attention

    d) All of the above

5. To what kind of game do the apologetics methods described in this course most closely resemble?

    a) A game of chess

    b) One-on-one basketball

    c) Ping-pong

    d) World War II

6. When it comes to defending against error, what is the very first line of defense God has given us?

    a) The Bible

    b) The Holy Spirit

    c) Our mind

    d) Our emotions

7. Why do some Christians get upset when you try to find the truth through argument and disagreement?

    a) They fear division

    b) They take all disagreement as hostility

    c) They value right living over right believing

    d) A and B

    e) A and C

8. No argument, act of love, or gospel presentation will be effective without:

    a) A listening ear

    b) A dose of humility

    c) Solid arguments

    d) The Holy Spirit

9. When it comes to the 100% God and 100% Man principle:

    a) I am not at all responsible for my side of the interaction, and God is entirely responsible for his

    b) I am wholly responsible for my side of the interaction, and God is not at all responsible for his

    c) I am only partly responsible for my side of the interaction, and God is only partly responsible for his

    d) I am wholly responsible for my side of the interaction, and God is entirely responsible for his

    e) None of the above

10. What is the goal when it comes to having conversations about Christianity with someone?

    a) To convert someone

    b) Put a bee in someone's bonnet

    c) To argue with someone

    d) Put a stone in someone's shoe

11. Most Christians should not try and close the deal and get people to respond to the gospel when it comes to conversations about the Christian faith, because:

    a) Most arguments will fall flat with people

    b) Not all Christians are good closers

    c) In most situations, the fruit is not ripe

    d) A and B

    e) B and C

12. What is true about how Greg responded to each of his four scenarios?

    a) He answered with a question

    b) His questions were invitations for dialogue

    c) His questions were asked with a purpose

    d) All of the above

13. What is key to the so-called Columbo tactic?

    a) To go on the offensive in an offensive way by using carefully selected questions to productively advance a conversation

    b) To go on the defensive in an inoffensive way by using carefully selected questions to productively advance an argument

    c) To go on the defensive in an offensive way by using carefully selected questions to productively advance a conversation

    d) To go on the offensive in an inoffensive way by using carefully selected questions to productively advance a conversation

14. Why does developing the habit of asking questions in spiritual conversations offer such a tremendous advantage?

    a) Questions are friendly; you'll get an education; you can make progress without being pushy

    b) Questions are backdoors to arguments; you'll get an education; you can make progress without being pushy

    c) Questions are friendly; you'll get a foot in the door with the gospel; you can make progress without being pushy

    d) Questions are friendly; you'll get an education; you can close the deal more quickly

15. What are the three basic ways to use the Columbo tactic?

    a) Gather information; reverse people's arguments; put yourself in control of the conversation

    b) Gather information; reverse the burden of proof; put yourself in control of the conversation

    c) Gather arguments; reverse the burden of proof; put yourself in control of the conversation

    d) Gather information; reverse the burden of proof; close the deal more quickly

Refining the Columbo Tactic (Chapters 4–5)

You Should Know

- "How did you come to that conclusion?" is the second Columbo question designed to enforce the burden-of-proof rule.

- "Is it possible?" reveals that some options seem completely unworkable on closer examination.

- "Is it plausible?" reveals that it's important to discern whether it is reasonable to think something might have taken place, given the evidence.

- "Is it probable?" reveals that we must be able to show why one view is more likely and better than another one, which requires reasons.

- Getting out of the hot seat is a way to manage a conversation when you sense you're overmatched, you decrease the pressure, research an issue, and rehearse a response.

- Burden of proof: the responsibility someone has to defend or give evidence for his view

- Alternative explanation: gives a different explanation to an argument, which isn't the same as giving an argument or refuting someone's argument

- Just so stories: an argument that offers a hypothetical explanation with a story of what might have taken place without giving actual facts

- Professor's ploy: a professor shifts the burden of proof from himself to someone else, demanding they defend views they haven't expressed

- Verbal aikido: using someone's aggressive conversational energy to your advantage by shifting from argument mode to fact-finding mode

- Passive-aggressive tolerance response: "Why is it when I think I'm right, I'm intolerant, but when you think you're right, you're just right?"

- Non sequitur: literally, "It does not follow," which is a reply that has a conclusion that does not follow from earlier statements

- Leading questions: questions designed to lead someone in the direction a person wants the conversation to go

Essay Questions
Short

1. Greg describes arguments like a simple house with a roof supported by walls. The roof is the conclusions, the walls are the supporting ideas. What ideas do you use to support your conclusions regarding the Christian faith?

2. Explain the differences between what is possible, plausible, and probable. Why are these differences important to keep in mind when discussing issues of faith?

3. How freeing is it to you to realize that you don't have to be the expert on every subject, but can keep the burden of proof on others to defend their claim? Why is the response, "Let me think about it," so useful in the midst of a conversation about your faith?

4. *The* question is "You're saying that people who don't believe just like you are going to hell?" What would be your answer if someone posed that question to you?

5. Greg reminds us that if we engage *the* question, we need to know *why* Jesus is the only way before it is helpful to tell people *that* he is the only way. Are you yourself secure in that knowledge? If not, what do you need to grow in that knowledge? If so, what would you want to communicate?

6. Have your convictions ever been labeled intolerant, bigoted, narrow-minded, or judgmental? If so, what was that like, and how did you respond? How might have using Columbo turned the tables in that conversation?

Long

1. Jesus tells us to be "as shrewd as snakes and as innocent as doves" (Matthew 10:16). What does he mean by this, and why is this import-ant in the midst of a conversation about your faith? How might it look in your life to follow Jesus' encouragement when you engage in spiritual conversations?

2. What do you think are some examples of the cherished views at stake that people hold about reality and spirituality — the kind where people raise objections that initially sound worthwhile, but simply can't be defended once examined? Offer three examples and explain why they can't be defended.

Quiz

1. Many challenges to Christianity thrive on vague generalities and forceful but vacuous slogans. The second step of Columbo will help. It's called:

    a) Reversing the Argument
    b) Reversing the Burden of Proof
    c) Reversing the Question
    d) None of the above

2. The so-called burden of proof rule can be summed up this way:

    a) Whoever makes the claim bears the burden
    b) Whoever offers proof wins the argument

   c) Whoever asks the question bears the burden to answer it

   d) None of the above

3. The first Columbo question helps you know *what* another person thinks. The second Columbo question helps you know:

   a) How he thinks the way he does

   b) Why he thinks the way he does

   c) Where he found what he thinks

   d) Who he thinks he is to say what he says

4. The question, "Now, how did you come to that conclusion?" accomplishes something vitally important by forcing persons you are in conversation with:

   a) To give an alternative explanation

   b) To ask questions about your beliefs

   c) To ask questions about their beliefs

   d) To give an account for their own beliefs

5. What three questions should you always ask whenever someone offers an explanation?

   a) Is it unworkable; unknowable; unreliable?

   b) Is it backwards; better; believable?

   c) Is it possible; plausible; probable?

   d) Is it acceptable; actual; articulate?

6. The goal of the so-called professor's ploy is to:

   a) Shift the burden of proof from the student to the professor

   b) Shift the burden of proof from the professor to the student

   c) Shift the burden of proof from the question to the answer

   d) Shift the burden of proof from the answer to the question

7. Instead of taking the bait of the professor ploy when you find yourself facing any form of the "Why don't you try to prove me wrong?" question, what should you do?

   a) Reframe the question in the form of an answer

   b) Withdraw the claim and move on to another apologetical tactic

    c) Shift the burden back to where it belongs, on the one who made the claim

    d) Take the burden back on yourself, rather than shift it to the one making the claim

8. When you don't have enough information to respond to a fast talker in an intense discussion, how can you respond?

    a) Don't feel pressure to immediately answer their points

    b) Say, "Let me think about it"

    c) Research the issue on your own, at your leisure

    d) Review and rehearse your response

    e) All of the above

9. On whose shoulders does the burden of proof belong?

    a) The one who is answering the challenge

    b) The one who is making the claim

    c) The one who is taking the claim

    d) No one is responsible

10. Every time you ask a question and get a favorable response, the person is telling you:

    a) He understands your point and disagrees with it provisionally

    b) He understands your point and agrees with it provisionally

    c) He misunderstands your point and doesn't like it

    d) He misunderstands your point, yet agrees with it

11. What is *the* question you'll be asked as you step out as an ambassador for Christ?

    a) You're saying that your way is the only way to God?

    b) You're saying that your religion is the only right one?

    c) You're saying that people who don't believe just like you are going to hell?

    d) All of the above

12. When it comes to engaging *the* question about belief and hell, when using the Columbo tactic there's a hitch:

    a) You have to know *why* Jesus is the only way before it is helpful to tell people *that* he is the only way

b) You have to know *who* Jesus is before it is helpful to tell people *why* he is

c) You have to know *that* Jesus is the only way before it is helpful to tell people *who* he is

d) None of the above

13. What bit of knowledge is key to the so-called passive-aggressive tolerance trick?

a) There is always neutral ground when it comes to issues of tolerance

b) There is usually some neutral ground when it comes to issues of tolerance

c) There is no neutral ground when it comes to issues of bigotry

d) There is no neutral ground when it comes to issues of tolerance

14. What is the danger of employing the third use of Columbo?

a) We become offensive when we go on the offensive

b) We become defensive when we go on the offensive

c) We become aggressive when we go on the offensive

d) We become passive when we go on the defensive

15. What question can you ask to soften your challenge in order to disagree with someone in an indirect approach?

a) "Have you considered . . . ?"

b) "Can you help me understand this?"

c) "Do you see how your argument doesn't work?"

d) A and B

e) A and C

Perfecting the Columbo Tactic (Chapter 6)

You Should Know

- Go out of your way to establish common ground, treating people the way you would like others to treat you, is a general rule for using Colombo.

- The purpose of our questions is to clarify issues in the discussion, clarify our points, or clarify some error we think the other person has made.

- When responding to leading questions, it is often important to say: "It seems you want to explain your point using questions. I'd rather you just state your own view directly."

- The response "What gives you the right to say someone else's religion is wrong?" really means: "No one is justified saying one religious view is better than another." Respond by saying, "What do you mean by that?"

- The respone "Who's to say?" really means: "No one could ever know the truth about that," or "One answer is just as good as another." The most important thing to remember is that behind the questions lurks strong opinions that are open to challenge if they can be flushed into the open.

- The response "Who are you to say?" really means: "You're wrong for saying someone else is wrong."

- Rejoinder: a counterargument the other side might make

- Improve Columbo skills: anticipate — consider conversations you might have about your convictions, anticipating obstacles you might encounter and Columbo questions in advance

- Improve Columbo skills: reflect — after conversations, take time to self-assess, asking how you did, how you could improve, and what you could do differently

- Improve Columbo skills: practice — consider new ideas or approaches, and practice it out loud, anticipating the twists and turns your new approach might take

- 2 things that give courage for conversations: preparation and action

- Third application of Columbo to guard against: leading questions from conversation partners

- Key to protecting yourself from Columbo abuse: Remember that you're in complete control of your side of the conversation; you have no obligation to cooperate with leading questions.

Essay Questions
Short

1. What sort of counterarguments do you think people might make toward you when you engage them in spiritual conversations? Write down a few examples so you can anticipate them next time.

2. What sorts of leading questions have you been asked in conversation with others about your faith? What could someone ask you that's such a question so you can be ready if they do?

3. What does the realization that you are in complete control of your own side of the conversation mean to you? How should this impact your conversations with others about your faith?

4. When have you been asked "What gives you the right . . . ?" or "Who are you to say . . . ?" How did those statement questions affect you or the conversation? What do you think was the point they were trying to make with their question?

5. What sorts of opinions would you say lurk behind the question "Who's to say?" In light of what you've learned, how can you respond when they arise?

6. How would you respond to the assertion, "Religions are basically the same"? What about "The Bible's been changed so many times"?

Long

1. Consider a new idea or approach to dialoguing with people about the Christian faith. Write it out, and then take time to practice it.

2. Explain the two Columbo executions in detail — halting, head-scratching, and harmless; confrontational and aggressive. Which do you resonate with the most? Why, and how can you employ it the next time you're in a conversation about your faith?

Quiz

1. When is the perfect time to focus on improving your Columbo technique?

   a) In the midst of your conversations
   b) At the beginning of the conversation
   c) At the end of the conversation
   d) Before the conversation begins and after it ends

2. What are three specific things you can do to ready yourself to respond to people in conversations?

   a) Anticipate beforehand what might come up
   b) Reflect afterwards on what took place
   c) Practice responses for the next conversation
   d) All of the above

3. What three skills of an ambassador are handy when it comes to focusing your reflection after a conversation?

   a) Knowledge, wisdom, and persuasion
   b) Knowledge, wisdom, and character

c) Gifts, wisdom, and character

d) Knowledge, revelation, and character

4. When you think of new ideas or approaches to conversing about the Christian faith:

a) Practice it out loud

b) Verify with some more reading

c) Go back to the drawing board

d) None of the above

5. What two things will help generate the courage you'll need to face a challenging situation?

a) Questions and answers

b) Arguments and verses

c) Preparation and action

d) Friends and family

6. As a general rule, when it comes to having apologetic conversations, whenever possible:

a) Make sure to prove your point and get them to agree

b) Affirm points of agreement between you and the other person

c) Take the most charitable read on other people's motives

d) A and B

e) B and C

7. What is the purpose of our questions?

a) Clarify the issues in the discussion

b) Clarify our points

c) Clarify some error we think the other person has made

d) All of the above

8. When someone begins using Columbo against us, there is a risk when they ask us:

a) To clarify our views

b) To give reasons for what we believe

c) Leading questions

d) All of the above

9. When you are asked leading questions, ask your dialogue partner:

   a) To simply state their own view directly
   b) To ask their question again
   c) To explain themselves
   d) To give you a break

10. For what reasons do people ask questions?

    a) They are curious or confused
    b) They want information
    c) They are rhetorical, designed to stimulate thinking
    d) They are challenging you
    e) All of the above

11. Why is the question, "What gives you the right . . . ?" not really a question?

    a) It's a poorly worded question
    b) It's a statement disguised as a question
    c) It's a leading question
    d) It's a rhetorical question

12. What do you want the person to do when they ask you a question disguised as a statement?

    a) Ask the question again
    b) Let you think about your answer
    c) Rephrase the question as a statement
    d) Give you the answer to their question

13. What is the most important thing to remember about the question "Who's to say?"

    a) Behind them are strong emotions that you should leave unchallenged and undiscovered
    b) Behind them is ignorance that should be questioned
    c) Behind them are stronger questions that can neither be answered nor challenged
    d) Behind them are strong opinions open to being challenged if brought into the open

14. What are the two basic executions of the Columbo tactic?

 a) Halting, head-scratching, and harmless; confrontational and aggressive
 b) Persuasive and opinionated; confrontational and aggressive
 c) Halting, head-scratching, and harmless; persuasive and opinionated
 d) Persuasive and opinionated; obstinate and rude

15. When people say to Christians, "Your narrow views are oppressive," or "The Bible's been changed so many times," or "All religions are basically the same," how should we respond?

 a) Retreat in silence
 b) Stand your ground
 c) Respond with, "I understand, and I'm sorry."
 d) Respond with, "Oh? How do you know?"

The Suicide Tactic (Chapters 7–9)

You Should Know

- Self-refuting views are ideas that defeat themselves, failing to meet their own criteria of validity.

- Law of noncontradiction: the common sense notion that contradictory statements cannot *both* be true at the same time

- A common attack on the Bible is the contention that men wrote the Bible and people are imperfect, therefore the Bible is flawed.

- Hinduism is a pantheistic Eastern religion that teaches "reality" is an illusion — *maya* — of which each of us is part.

- The tactical goal of suicide tactics is to show the person that there is a fatal inconsistency in his beliefs.

- Suicide tactic: a tactic that leverages the rule of noncontradiction to expose how a view defeats itself by expressing contradictory concepts

- Formal suicide: an idea or objection that violates the law of noncontradiction in a straightforward fashion

- Necessarily false: the view that something cannot be true in any possible way, which makes defending them a lost caused

- Religious pluralism suicide: If all religions are true, then Christianity is true; religions have diverse pictures of the spiritual realm.

- Scientism: Knowledge begins and ends with the scientific method — and anything else is mere opinion and unsubstantiated belief.

- Practical suicide: views that simply cannot work in real-life application

- Determinism: Freedom is an illusion, choices are determined by circumstances preceding them and the result of blind physical forces beyond control.

- Sibling rivalry: a person raising two objections that are at odds with each other

- Scientific suicide: The truths science needs cannot be established by the method of science; it cannot operate in a vacuum.

Essay Questions

Short

1. What statements have you heard that fail the law of noncontradiction test? In what way do those statements self-destruct because of internal contradiction?

2. When have you encountered the notion of religious pluralism? How might you respond in light of this session?

3. In what ways have you seen moral relativism taking hold of our culture? Why do you think their view of reality is so destructive, and how have you noticed its destruction?

4. What is the so-called Sibling Rivalry Suicide? How might you respond the next time you encounter that argument?

5. Why is the existence of evil powerful evidence *for* God, not against him? How might this insight aid you in your conversations with people?

6. What is *scientism*? When have you encountered it before? In light of this lesson, how can you show how scientism self-destructs?

Long

1. Paul warned, "See to it that no one takes you captive through hollow and deceptive philosophy, which depends on human tradition and the

elemental spiritual forces of this world rather than on Christ" (Colossians 2:8). What hollow and deceptive philosophies are all the rage in our day that are taking people captive? List three examples, and how you can be a refuge from such error.

2. Greg insists that the Suicide tactic isn't an end of itself, but can be used as a bridge to further questions. Why might this be important to keep in mind as you dialogue with people? Now, chose one of those tactics and write out a script for how you can refute an idea with it.

Quiz

1. An idea or objection that violates the law of noncontradiction in a straightforward fashion is called:
   a) Formal suicide
   b) Informal suicide
   c) Informed suicide
   d) Uninformed suicide

2. To recognize if a view has suicidal tendencies:
   a) Pay attention to the basic idea, premise, conviction, or claim
   b) Ask if the claim applies to itself. If so, is there a conflict?
   c) Simply point out the contradiction
   d) All of the above

3. The argument against God based on the existence of evil is popular precisely because:
   a) It addresses something we all wonder about
   b) It trades on a presumed contradiction
   c) It trades on a presumed noncontradiction
   d) It addresses something none of us believe

4. What kind of question is "Can God make a rock so big that he can't lift it?"
   a) A self-defeating question
   b) A nonsensical question
   c) A pseudo-question
   d) A fallacious question

5. If we can't believe in religion, why shouldn't we believe science either?
   a) Because there is no biblical evidence for it
   b) Because there is no scientific evidence for it
   c) Because there is no existential evidence for it
   d) None of the above

6. "It's wrong to say people are wrong" is an example of what kind of suicidal statement?
   a) Formal suicide
   b) Practical suicide
   c) Experiential suicide
   d) Relative suicide

7. Who are especially vulnerable to practical suicide?
   a) Christians
   b) Americans
   c) Moral relativists
   d) All of the above

8. How can we respond to people when they say, "You shouldn't force your morality on other people"?
   a) "You're right."
   b) "If you think it's wrong, then why are you doing it yourself?"
   c) "Why not?"
   d) B and C

9. People who claim it is wrong to change other people's religious beliefs are usually guilty of committing what kind of suicide?
   a) Formal suicide
   b) Practical suicide
   c) Experiential suicide
   d) Relative suicide

10. In practice, arguments for determinism are:
   a) Non sequiturs
   b) Self-defeating
   c) Self-obvious
   d) None of the above

11. What is the type of suicide moral relativists commit when they object to the problem of evil?

    a) Formal suicide
    b) Practical suicide
    c) Sibling rivalry
    d) Infanticide

12. When it comes to the problem of evil, what two rival concepts do moral relativists promote?

    a) Subjective morality and objective evil
    b) Subjective evil and objective morality
    c) Personal views and preferences
    d) Biblical views and reality

13. What does the example "Son, if you didn't get this letter, please let me know, and I'll send another. I made a copy" illustrate?

    a) Formal suicide
    b) Practical suicide
    c) Sibling rivalry
    d) Infanticide

14. When it comes to the problem of evil, one must first know

    a) What evil is before one can point to examples of it
    b) Examples of evil before one can point to it
    c) Why evil exists before one can talk about it
    d) Who is evil before one can point to it

15. With the infanticide type of suicide, the notion of morality (with its corresponding concept of evil) rests upon the prior foundation of:

    a) God's actions
    b) Human actions
    c) God's existence
    d) Human existence

The Taking-the-Roof-Off Tactic (Chapter 10)

You Should Know

- Someone's idea of what the world is like is their worldview.

- The appeal to nature and homosexuality states that anything that is natural is also moral. Homosexuality is natural, as the claim goes, therefore, homosexuality is moral.

- When using "trotting out the toddler" response to abortion, you ask if a woman should have the right to kill her one-year-old. It reveals that logic of choice, privacy, and rights endangers newborns as much as the unborn.

- The notion that faith is believing things we cannot know is an unbiblical view of faith.

- Moral motivation for Earth Day only makes sense if there's a God who entrusted man with Earth's stewardship.

- When responding to the statement "That's just your interpretation," discover if the person thinks all interpretations are equal and yours is just an alternative, and then ask how you've distorted Scripture.

- Taking the Roof Off: designed to show that some views are too much, and if taken seriously, they lead to counterintuitive, absurd results

- Reductio ad absurdum: means to reduce a point to its absurd conclusions

- Roof removal steps: reduce point of view to its argument; see where it leads; invite them to consider the view's implications

- Response to, "If Jesus would forgive capital criminals, then it is wrong to execute them": even though *Jesus* might forgive murderers, that does not mean it is wrong for the *government* to punish them

- Response to, "Because people were wrong in the past on slavery, they are wrong in the present on homosexuality": just because people were wrong in the past about slavery doesn't mean they are now wrong about same-sex marriage

- Response to, "Any 'natural' tendency or behavior is morally acceptable": just because an impulse is natural does not mean it's moral. Homosexuality cannot be justified this way.

- Apologia: a defense for our hope with evidence and facts

- Response to modified pro-choice position: "You're convinced abortion kills an innocent child, yet you think laws should allow women to do that to their own babies?"

Essay Questions

Short

1. What is a worldview? Offer a complete example to illustrate.

2. Why is it true that if you start with relativism, reality doesn't make sense? Explain.

3. "Just because an impulse is natural does not mean it's moral." What other "natural" impulses that are also destructive and immoral do people have that you could use to support this claim?

4. Have you encountered anyone justifying abortion by saying, "Women have the right to choose"? What was that conversation like? How might the insights from this lesson guide future conversations?

5. Who do you know who has a deep moral concern about the environment? How might you use Greg's arguments that "Earth Day makes sense for theists, but not Darwinists" on page 154 in a conversation with them about faith?

6. Why is it true that there actually *are* interpretations that are better than others? Do you believe this? Why or why not? Provide an example to illustrate the truth of this statement.

Long

1. What do you think about the contemporary argument that because people were wrong in the past about slavery and interracial marriage they are wrong in the present about gay marriage? Explain that argument, then write out a detailed response to use next time you hear it.

2. Explain the idea that "Faith and knowledge are not opposites in Scripture. They are companions. The opposite of faith is not fact, but unbelief. The opposite of knowledge is ignorance"? Why do you think this might be important to your conversations about faith?

Quiz

1. Someone's map of reality, their idea of what the world is like, is called:

   a) A worldview
   b) A planner
   c) A method
   d) None of the above

2. The Taking-the-Roof-Off tactic is also known as *reductio ad absurdum*, which means:

   a) It does not follow
   b) It follows deduction
   c) To reduce a point to its absurd conclusions
   d) To follow the clues to their logical conclusions

3. What powerful ally do Christians have in the war of ideas?

   a) Arguments
   b) Reality
   c) The Bible
   d) Proofs

4. Anyone who denies the truth of God's world lives in a:
   a) Fantasy
   b) Lie
   c) Contradiction
   d) Glass house

5. The key to dealing with moral relativism is realizing that for all the adamant affirmations,
   a) No one really believes it
   b) No one really understands it
   c) Everyone accepts it
   d) Everyone lives it

6. When it comes to responding to moral relativism we should start with:
   a) Guilt, then reason forward to acts of evil
   b) Guilt, then reason back to the Bible
   c) Guilt, then reason forward to the Christian faith
   d) Guilt, then reason back to morality and a moral lawgiver

7. What are the steps to using Taking the Roof Off?
   a) Reduce the person's point of view to its basic argument
   b) Give the idea a test drive to see where the argument leads
   c) If you find out a problem, point it out and invite the person to consider the implications
   d) All of the above

8. How can the "born bad" argument be basically summarized?
   a) Anything that I like to do is moral
   b) Anything that is natural is moral
   c) Anything that makes me happy is moral
   d) None of the above

9. What do some people think make faith impossible?
   a) Experience and emotion
   b) Experience and knowledge
   c) Facts and emotion
   d) Facts and knowledge

10. Faith and knowledge are not opposites in Scripture. Instead they are:

   a) Conflicting
   b) Companions
   c) Unknowable
   d) None of the above

11. The opposite of faith is:

   a) Unbelief
   b) Fact
   c) Dogma
   d) Doubt

12. The opposite of knowledge is:

   a) Faith
   b) Unbelief
   c) Ignorance
   d) Dogma

13. What will people often say to parry your argument when you make a biblical point?

   a) "That's not what the Bible says!"
   b) "That's just your interpretation!"
   c) "That's not reliable!"
   d) "That's fine for you to believe!"

14. "Faith is believing things we cannot know" is what kind of understanding of faith?

   a) Simplistic
   b) Theological
   c) Emotional
   d) Biblical

15. What do people erect that the Taking the Roof Off tactic tries to remove?

   a) A story to immerse to reinforce their beliefs
   b) A list to remind themselves of the logical implications of what they don't believe

c) A self-deception to shield themselves from the logical implications of their beliefs

d) Self-doubt to encourage themselves to challenge what others believe

1. A, 2. C, 3. B, 4. C, 5. A, 6. D, 7. D, 8. B, 9. D, 10. B, 11. A, 12. C, 13. B, 14. D, 15. C

The Steamroller Tactic (Chapters 11–14)

You Should Know

- Barriers to belief: rational reasons, emotional reasons, prejudice, and pigheadedness

- Steamrollers: people who try to overpower you with the force of their personality

- Characteristics of steamrollers: aggressive, constantly interrupt, pile on other challenges, change the subject, never listen

- 3 steps to stopping a steamroller: stop the interruption and negotiate an agreement; shame him by making a direct request for courtesy; leave the conversation

- Ricochet evangelism: when the Holy Spirit has a different audience in mind for your gospel efforts than your dialogue partner

- Rhodes Scholar tactic: reveals if an appeal to an authority is legitimate by getting past their *opinion* and probing *reasons* for them

- Fallacy of expert witness: relying on authorities who give opinions that are outside of their area of expertise

- Naturalistic materialism: a scientific philosophy saying all phenomena must be explained in terms of matter and energy governed by natural law

- The historical Jesus: a school of thought where scholars try to distinguish the Jesus of history from the miracle-working Jesus of faith

- Just-the-Facts tactic: a simple appeal to facts in order to bring awareness to challenges to Christianity based on bad information

- 2 steps of Just-the-Facts tactic: first ask, "What is the claim?" Then ask, "Is the claim factually accurate?"

- Ideological self-preservation: intellectually circling the wagons and guarding against the slightest challenge to our beliefs in the interest of providing security

- Elements of the Ambassador's Creed: An ambassador is . . . ready, patient, reasonable, tactical, clear, fair, honest, humble, attractive, and dependent.

Essay Questions

Short

1. In what way are rational reasons a barrier to belief? What are some of those rational reasons?

2. What are the three steps Greg outlines for dealing with steamrollers? In what way do you think they would be effective, and how would they free you in the midst of spiritual conversations with such people?

3. When you face an aggressive challenger, Greg encourages us to give them the last word. Why do you think this is sound advice, and what might it do for spiritual conversations?

4. Greg suggests that scientific evidence could, in principle, indicate someone who created the universe, rather than it springing from chance. What evidence have you encountered that seems to make this case, that belief in a Creator is more than mere faith?

5. Do you have any people in your life that could be your "little platoon" to help you make a difference? How might it look in your life to start a modest fire with a cluster of believers of kindred spirit who value using their minds in their pursuit of God to engage people in spiritual conversations?

6. Read through the Ambassador's Creed again on pages 199–200. How can you live out the points of this creed in order to engage people in spiritual conversations most effectively?

Long

1. Greg points us to two slogans of the U.S. Marine Corp.: "Always Prepared" and "The more you sweat in training, the less you bleed in battle." How prepared would you say you are for spiritual conversations? Take an inventory of areas of strength and weakness, and consider how you could sweat more in training so that you bleed less in battle.

2. Consider the story Greg told about the Jehovah's Witnesses missionaries on pages 194–196. How would you describe your own confidence in your message, interest in the salvation of others, and how seriously you take truth? What do you need in order to gain confidence and grow in all three?

Quiz

1. Why do people have emotional reasons for ignoring your points?
   a) Many have had annoying experiences with Christianity
   b) Some have been part of abusive churches
   c) They would have to admit cherished dead loved ones entered eternity without forgiveness and with a fate of suffering
   d) All of the above

2. Key to the first step dealing with a steamroller, especially with aggressive ones, is to:
   a) Get them to back off
   b) Get them sidetracked
   c) Get verbal consent to your argument
   d) Get verbal consent to your request for courtesy

3. When taking the second step with a steamroller:
   a) Ignore them completely and leave
   b) Ignore any new challenges he has introduced; make your arguments again more forcefully

    c) Ignore any new challenges he has introduced; shame him by making an explicit request for courtesy

    d) Engage the new challenges he has introduced; offer convincing proofs to answer them point by point

4. When all else fails with a steamroller:

    a) Let go of your feelings and let him talk

    b) Try again with your main argument

    c) Repeat your request for courtesy one more time

    d) Let it go and walk away

5. How do you know when someone has crossed the line, and when should we save the "pearls" of our message for another time? When they show:

    a) They aren't interested in the precious gift being offered them

    b) They have utter contempt for the precious gift being offered them

    c) They don't understand the precious gift being offered them

    d) All of the above

6. What is key to the Rhodes Scholar tactic?

    a) Always asking for facts, not settling for reasons

    b) Always asking for reasons, not settling for facts

    c) Always asking for opinions, not settling for facts

    d) Always asking for reasons, not settling for opinions

7. What should you ask when people appeal to authority?

    a) "Why should I believe this person's motives?"

    b) "Why should I believe this person's opinion?"

    c) "Why should I believe this argument's facts?"

    d) All of the above

8. The popular complaint "Creation is not science" capitalizes on an ambiguity between two different definitions of science. What are they?

    a) Scientific methodology and naturalistic science

    b) Scientific equations and naturalistic science

    c) Scientific methodology and naturalistic spirituality

    d) Scientific spirituality and naturalistic impulses

9. Whenever someone uses the word "scientific" to describe the way they look at history, what are they signaling governs the process?

    a) Materialistic philosophy
    b) Methodological science
    c) Christian spirituality
    d) None of the above

10. What two things are consistent with the worldview of the theist?

    a) Laws of God and supernatural intervention
    b) Laws of spirituality and natural intervention
    c) Laws of science and natural intervention
    d) Laws of nature and supernatural intervention

11. Facts show that the greatest evil has always resulted from:

    a) Pursuit of God, not denial of him
    b) Pursuit of faith, not denial of faith
    c) Denial of God, not pursuit of him
    d) Denial of humanity, not pursuit of it

12. What is an important element of the Just the Facts tactic?

    a) Persuasion
    b) Precision
    c) Profession
    d) Purpose

13. Before beginning any research using the Just the Facts tactic, ask the question:

    a) "Does anything about the assertion seem suspicious or unlikely on its face?"
    b) "Does anything about the assertion seem sound and likely on its face?"
    c) "Does anything about the assertion seem factually accurate on its face?"
    d) "Does anything about the assertion seem like he knows what he's talking about on its face?"

14. Instead of focusing on the benefits of Christianity, we should focus on its:

a) Truth
b) Possibility
c) Features
d) Satisfactions

15. If people want to leave our conversations, we should let them. But we shouldn't let them leave:

a) With unanswered questions
b) With the last word
c) Having won
d) Empty-handed

Notes

www.ingramcontent.com/pod-product-compliance
Lightning Source LLC
Chambersburg PA
CBHW010038040426
42331CB00037B/3308